300
GEOGRAPHY FACTS
FOR KIDS

KENTISH PRESS

300
Geography facts for kids

KENTISH PRESS ARE AN INDEPENDENT SELF-PUBLISHING TEAM COMMITTED TO PRODUCING THE BEST QUALITY BOOKS POSSIBLE.

ALL INFORMATION IN THIS BOOK IS CORRECT AT THE TIME OF PUBLICATION (MAY 2022), BUT IF YOU NOTICE ANYTHING THAT DOESN'T SEEM RIGHT AT THE TIME OF USING THE BOOK THEN PLEASE LET US KNOW AT KENTISHPRESS@GMAIL.COM AND WE WILL BE HAPPY TO HELP.

KENTISH PRESS

KENTISH PRESS

IF YOU ENJOY THIS BOOK AND WOULD LIKE TO CHECK OUT MORE OF OUR OTHER BOOKS THEN SCAN THE QR CODE BELOW.

WE HAVE A NUMBER OF FACT BOOKS FOR KIDS INCLUDING FOOTBALL FACTS, HISTORY FACTS AND MUCH MORE.

ALTERNATIVELY YOU CAN SEARCH FOR 'KENTISH PRESS' ON AMAZON

SCAN ME

WE HOPE YOU ENJOY THE BOOK!!

KENTISH PRESS

Sections Within This Book

Countries and Continents

Weather and Climate

Volcanoes and Mountains

Oceans, Lake and Rivers

Urbanisation and population

Coasts

Natural Disasters

The Earth

Rocks and Soil

Countries and Continents

Countries and Continents

Of the 7 continents, Asia is the biggest. It covers over 44 million kilometres squared.

The largest country in the world is Russia. Russia covers an area of 17.1 million kilometres squared.

The continent that has the most countries within it is Africa. Africa contains 54 different countries.

The smallest country in the world is Vatican City which is estimated to have a population of less than 1,000 individuals.

The Earth previously consisted of one "supercontinent" called Pangea. Due to plate tectonics the Earth now has 7 separate continents.

The continents are currently shifting around the Earth at a rate similar to that at which your fingernails are growing.

The continent of Africa is the only continent on Earth that covers all 4 of the hemispheres.

Alaska, a state in the United States of America, is both the westernmost and easternmost state.

Of the 24 time zones in the world, Russia uses 11. One side of Russia may be going to bed, whilst the other side is getting out of bed. This demonstrates the sheer size of the country.

Due to owning many different overseas territories, the country of France has the most time zones in the world, with 12.

When we think of the word "pyramid" our minds often think of the country of Egypt. However, Sudan has many more pyramids than Egypt.

The most remote place in the world is a place named "Point Nemo". This place is roughly 1,000 miles away from any other piece of land.

The most linguistically diverse country is Papua New Guinea. Here they have 840 different spoken languages.

In the continent of South America there are only 2 countries that do not border Brazil - these are Chile and Ecuador.

There are 195 countries in the world.

Worried about getting bitten by mosquitoes when you go on holiday? Look no further than Iceland. This is the only country where no mosquitoes can be found.

China is the country with the most bordering countries - there are 14.

The language that is spoken by the highest number of people around the world is Mandarin. It is spoken by over 1 billion people.

The longest international border is shared between the United States of America and Canada. It is 8,890 kilometres long.

The country of Australia is wider than the moon.

The country of Nauru is the only country that does not possess an official capital city.

Despite what you may think, at the closest point, the distance between the USA and Russia is a mere 3.8 kilometres.

There is a city named Rome on every continent in the world except for Antarctica.

Istanbul is the only city whose location spans across two different continents - Europe and Asia.

Even though the territory covering China is within 5 different time zones, China only uses 1 time zone for the entire country.

There are 11 states in the United States of America that are bigger than the United Kingdom.

The largest producer and exporter of mangoes in the world is in Asia - India to be precise.

There are more billionaires in Asia than in any other continent.

90% of the world's rice is consumed in countries within the continent of Asia.

Algeria is the largest country in mainland Africa. You can also find part of the Sahara Desert here.

The smallest country in Africa is an island nation named the Seychelles.

The most widely spoken language in the continent of Africa is Arabic.

The country of Morocco is home to the oldest educational institution that is still operating - The University of Karueein.

Oceania is the smallest of the continents and is comprised of 14 countries.

Before 1840, the continent of Antarctica possessed a different name - Terra Australis Incognita. This translates as "the unknown land of the South".

The continent of Antarctica plays an important role in protecting the Earth from global warming. This is because the large ice sheet helps to reflect away solar radiation from the Earth's surface.

There is no time zone in Antarctica. Individuals use the time zone of their research station or the country that is located closest to where they are.

The name "Europe" is thought by some to mean "the woman with large eyes".

Europe possesses both the smallest country in the world (Vatican City) and the largest country in the world (Russia).

Wine is loved around Europe. The top 3 exporters of wine are all found in Europe: Italy, France and Spain.

If you are in France and you own a pig, do not call it Napoleon. By doing so you could find yourself with some jail time!

South America was discovered by an Italian explorer with the name of Amerigo Vespucci.

La Paz is the capital of Bolivia, and it is the highest capital city in the world, sitting at an altitude of 3,625 metres above sea level.

The 4 largest cities in the United States are all located in the state of Alaska.

In Texas there is a ranch (King Ranch) that is bigger than the entire state of Rhode Island.

There are 3 countries in the world that are completely landlocked by another country. These countries are San Marino, Vatican City and Lesotho.

Iceland provides its residents with free heat for their homes using geothermal energy.

It is possible for Ireland to grow palm trees at 55 degrees North. This is due to help from the warm ocean currents.

Sweden is the country that possesses the greatest number of islands. It has 267,000 of them!

There are 26 cities in the world whose names are just 1 letter long.

The most popular name for a city in the USA is "Franklin". There are a total of 31 cities with this name.

The colour that appears on the most national flags is red. The colour red appears on 155 national flags in total.

To get from Norway to North Korea you would only have to cross one other country.

Perhaps surprisingly, the longest border that France shares with another country is with Brazil. This is due to French Guyana.

Portugal is split by the Tagus River, which separates the north and south of the country.

Pheasant Island, which is located in Europe's Bidasoa River, is occupied by both France and Spain. They switch ownership of the island every 6 months.

Weather and Climate

Weather and Climate

The hottest temperature ever recorded on Earth is 56.7 Celsius. This was recorded in Death Valley, California in 1913.

The coldest temperature ever recorded on Earth at ground level is minus 89.2 Celsius. This was in Antarctica

The fastest wind speed ever recorded was in Australia in 1996. The wind speed was recorded at 254 miles per hour!

Most people think a desert needs to be a hot climate. However, a desert is an area of land where little rain or snow occurs, making it inhospitable for animals to live. Some deserts can be found in Antarctica and are very cold.

The hottest average temperature in an inhabited place on Earth is found in Dallol, Ethiopia. Temperatures average a scorching 41.1 Celsius.

The coldest average temperature on Earth is found in Oymyakon, Russia, where winter temperatures average around minus 50 Celsius.

The wettest place on Earth is a village in India named Mawsynram, which has an average of 1,839 centimetres of rain each year.

A hurricane and a typhoon are the same phenomenon; however, they are called a different name depending on the location.

China suffers the most typhoons (hurricanes) in the world. In the last 52 years they have had over 172 of them.

Every minute on Earth there are roughly 2,000 thunderstorms occurring.

Sometimes in Antarctica, the snow falls so hard that it is not possible to see your hand in front of your face.

Fire whirls can be created during wildfires. These are small tornado-like phenomena that are made of fire.

One of the most damaging thunderstorms that ever occurred was in Texas in the year 1995. During this thunderstorm, hailstones the size of cricket balls fell from the sky.

During the year of 1684, the river Thames in London froze for a period of 2 months due to the cold temperatures.

Hurricanes rotate around a circular centre that is known as "the eye". The eye of the storm is often very calm, and little wind occurs inside it.

Fortunately, most hurricanes occur out at sea and cause little damage. However, when hurricanes reach land, this is where a lot of damage and destruction may happen.

Hurricanes rotate in different directions depending which hemisphere they are in. This is due to something named "the Coriolis force".

The largest hurricane ever recorded was named Typhoon Tip and it possessed a diameter of over 2,200 kilometres.

The highest temperature that was ever recorded in Antarctica was 15 degrees Celsius - still not quite shorts and t-shirt weather!

A lightning strike travels at a speed of around 270,000 miles per hour.

Although thunder and lightning seems like a relatively rare occurrence, lightning strikes the Earth about 44 times every second.

The area on Earth that receives the most lightning strikes is Lake Maracaibo in Venezuela. In this location, thunderstorms occur about 150 days of the year.

Helicopters can cause lightning strikes. When a helicopter is flying it creates a negative charge. When the helicopter flies into a region of positive charge, this can create a lightning strike.

The average length of a lightning strike is between 2-3 miles. However, the width of a lightning strike is usually just a few centimetres.

Volcanic eruptions can cause lightning to occur. The earth and the ash that are in the air crash together and cause an electrical charge. An imbalance in these charges can create lightning strikes.

Lightning strikes are hot! Lightning bolts can reach temperatures of up to 29,982 degrees Celsius.

It used to be widely believed that bell ringing would prevent thunderstorms. However, bell ringing to prevent storms was banned in the 1800s due to over a hundred deaths when the bell ringers would climb up to the high metal tower and get struck by lightning.

Each year, lightning claims the lives of about 2,000 people. It is always safer to be indoors when there is a thunderstorm present.

The average lightning strike releases enough energy to power a 100-watt lightbulb for 3 months.

In 1955, a thunderstorm set off some Belgian explosives that were buried after the war. Fortunately, the only casualty from this explosion was one cow.

Lebanon is the only state in the Middle East where there is no desert.

The Sahara Desert experienced snowfall in February 1979.

The highest dew point ever recorded was in Saudi Arabia in 2003. The dew point recorded was 35 degrees Celsius.

It is possible to tell what the temperature is by counting the number of chirps from a cricket in 14 seconds.

Sandstorms occur when winds pick up and carry huge volumes of sand and dirt in the air. They can reach over 300 metres in height and have wind speeds of up to 25 miles per hour.

Sandstorms can cause lots of damage and are said to cause respiratory trouble in individuals who experience them, due to high amounts of sand and dirt getting into the body.

The highest wind speed ever recorded was in Barrow Island, Australia. A wind speed of 253 miles per hour was recorded during a tropical cyclone.

Wildfires are primarily caused by humans, with an estimated 90% of all wildfires said to have been started due to human action.

It is estimated that over 1.2 million acres of woodland burn every year in the USA alone, due to wildfires.

For snow to form there must be dust or pollen present in the air. This is needed for the creation of ice crystals.

Although it is not that likely, snow can fall in temperatures above freezing. This is much more likely to happen when the air is very dry, and the snowfall is heavy.

It is possible for the temperature to be too warm to snow, however it is not possible for it to be too cold to snow.

Most snowflakes travel down from the sky at speeds of between 1 and 4 miles per hour.

The average snowflake takes an hour to reach the ground after it is formed.

Volcanoes and Mountains

Volcanoes and mountains

The tallest mountain is called Mount Everest, standing a whopping 8,489 metres above sea level.

The longest mountain range on Earth is the mid-ocean ridge. This mountain range spans just under 65,000 kilometres. However, much of this mountain range is under water.

The longest mountain range that is above sea level is the Andes. The Andes can be found in South America and is around 7,000 kilometres in length.

Mount Thor, in Canada, has the highest vertical drop in the world. The drop is just over 1,250 metres down.

There is a mountain taller than Mount Everest, however as its base begins below sea level, it is not considered the tallest mountain. The name of this mountain is Mauna Kea and in total its height is about 10,000 metres.

Volcanoes can be found on the ocean floor as well as on ice caps.

Roughly 90% of all the volcanoes on Earth can be found in a place named the "Ring of Fire". This is an area found in the Pacific Ocean.

Apart from the vast number of volcanoes that can be found on the ocean floor, there are about 1,350 volcanoes that are potentially active around the world.

The word 'volcano' originates from Vulcan, the Roman god of fire.

Approximately 350 million people live in an area close to an active volcano that is considered a danger area.

Volcanoes can come in a wide range of shapes, but there are 2 main types. Composite volcanoes are cone shaped and have steep sides. Shield volcanoes are wide and have gently sloped sides.

Magma and lava are not the same thing. Magma is the hot liquid rock that is inside the volcano. It is not called lava until it has reached the outside of the volcano.

Lava can reach incredibly high temperatures, with estimates suggesting the temperature can reach up to 1,250 degrees Celsius.

The largest currently active volcano can be found in Hawaii. It is named Mauna Loa and it stands at 4,169 metres tall.

Volcanoes are not just found on our planet. Other planets have volcanoes. The largest volcano in our solar system is on Mars, and is called Olympus Mons.

The Appalachian Mountains used to be as tall as the Rocky Mountains. However, the Appalachian Mountains are now smaller because they are shrinking.

The tallest volcano is called Ojos de Salado. Is is located in Chile and measures 6,893 metres high. This volcano is dormant.

19 of the top 25 highest peaks in the world can all be found in the Himalayas.

The tallest mountain in Europe is called Mount Elbrus. This mountain is found in Russia and is 5,642 metres tall.

The top of Mount Everest is formed from a rock called marine limestone. This rock originated in a shallow sea in the Indian Ocean.

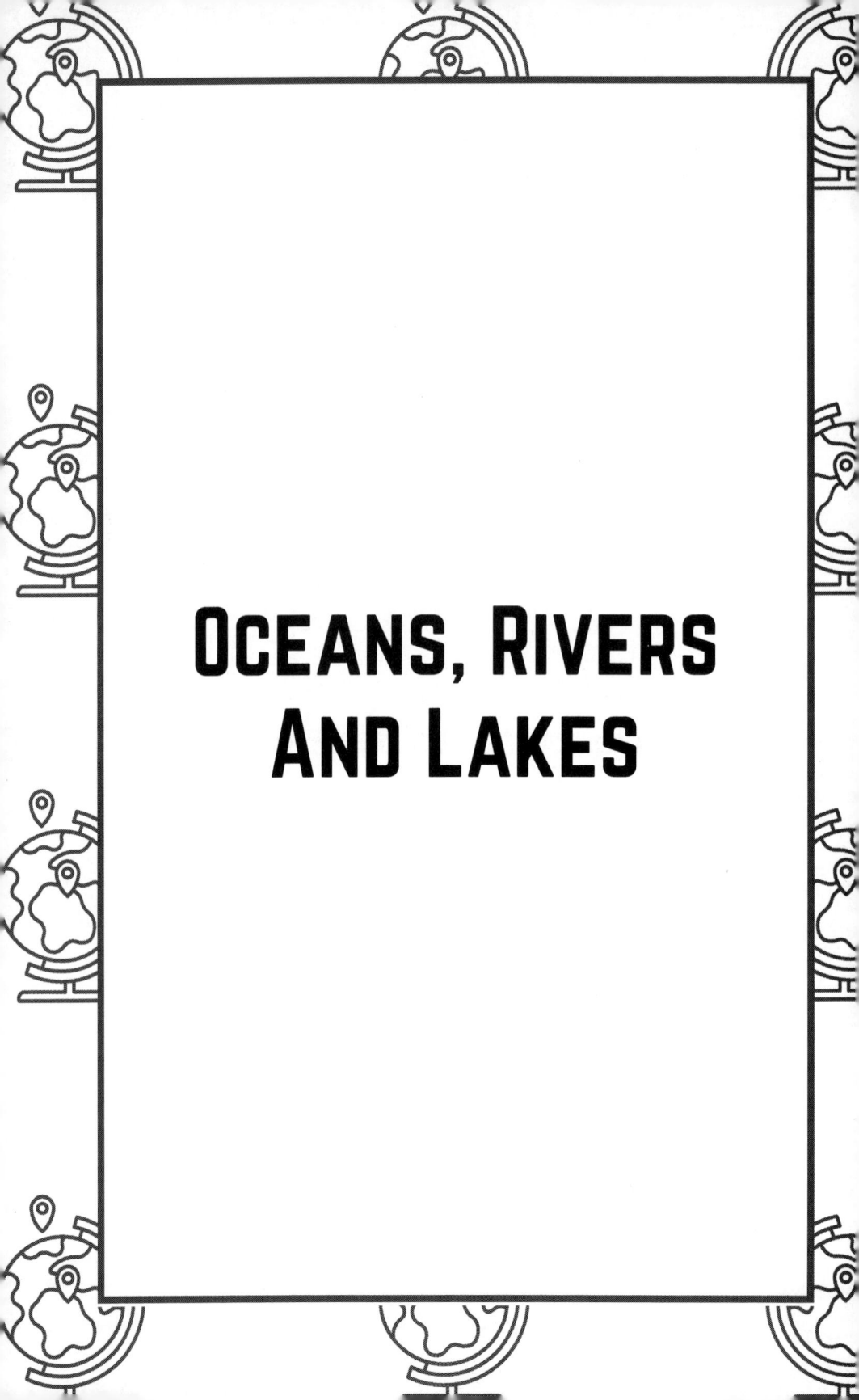

Oceans, Rivers And Lakes

Oceans, Rivers and Lakes

The largest ocean on Earth is called the Pacific Ocean. This ocean covers a staggering 63 million kilometres squared.

The Dead Sea is a salt lake that consists of such high levels of salt that individuals can float on the water's surface.

Although it may not seem like it due to living on land much of the time, over 70% of the Earth's surface is water.

Almost all of Earth's fresh water is held in Antarctica.

There is one sea, called the Sargasso Sea, that has no coasts. It is a floating sea that is there due to several different ocean currents.

Due to high concentrations of salt forming on the ocean floors, it is possible for underwater lakes and rivers to form.

The deepest part of the ocean is so deep that the tallest mountain in the world, Mount Everest, would be able to fit inside it.

The Amazon River, in South America, is recognised as the world's longest river. The Amazon is 4,345 miles long.

The deepest lake in the world is Lake Baikal in Russia. It boasts depths of up to 1,642 metres.

The Pacific Ocean makes up one third of the entire Earth.

Although coral reefs may just seem like pretty, colourful rocks, they are actually living creatures called coral.

The largest reef system in the world is named the Great Barrier Reef. This reef can even be seen from space.

The name for the Pacific Ocean comes from the Latin "Tepre Pacificum". This translates as "peaceful sea".

Only about 5% of the Earth's oceans have been explored.

Although the Nile River is commonly associated with Egypt, the Nile flows through a total of eleven countries in Africa.

The longest river in Europe is called the Volga River. This river is 3,685 kilometres long, and it flows through Russia.

The world's oceans contain over 326 million trillion gallons of water!

Whilst tap water would freeze at 0 degrees Celsius, sea water would need to be at a temperature of minus 2 degrees Celsius to freeze. This is due to its salt content.

The primary reason why the ocean and the sea appear blue in colour is due to the way in which water molecules absorb and scatter the light rays from the sun.

There are more historical artefacts underneath the surface of the Earth's oceans than there are in all of the world's museums.

Most of the data that is transferred internationally is done so by very large wires underneath the ocean.

The water pressure at the bottom of the ocean would be enough to crush a human body.

Oceans have a lot of gold in them. In fact, the estimated worth of gold in the oceans is said to be around $770 trillion.

There are only two countries within the continent of South America that do not border the ocean: Bolivia and Paraguay.

The Red Sea is the warmest sea in the world, with surface water temperatures sometimes reaching 30 degrees Celsius.

The Arctic Ocean is the shallowest and the smallest ocean on planet Earth.

Canada has more lakes than the rest of the world combined.

The volume of water in the Amazon River is greater than the volume of water in the next 8 largest rivers combined.

The Dead Sea is located at a depth of 400 metres below sea level.

In the year 2000, a new ocean was introduced by the International Hydrographic Organization. It's called the Southern Ocean and it surrounds Antarctica.

The Amazon River does not have a single bridge to cross it.

There are underwater hot springs in oceans that can reach temperatures of over 340 degrees Celsius.

Brazil has the most fresh water compared to any other country. This is largely due to the Amazon region.

Currently, scientists are aware of about 240,000 different marine species in our oceans. However, it is estimated that there are over 1 million.

Vulcan Point is an island that is within a lake, on an island, that is within a lake, on an island. You may need to read that a few times!

The deepest river is the Congo River in Africa. The deepest part of this river is 230 metres. However, scientists say that some parts of the river may be even deeper than this.

Saudi Arabia has no rivers.

Urbanisation and Population

Urbanisation and Population

Over 90% of the world's population live in the Northern Hemisphere of the Earth.

There are 42 buildings in New York City that have their own postcode/zip code. Some examples of these are the Empire State Building and the Chrysler Building.

Although much smaller in size, the state of California has a higher population than the country of Canada. As of 2019, California had a population of 39.75 million, whilst Canada had a population of 37.5 million.

There is a town in Nebraska, USA called Monowi. This town only has one single resident.

During the football world cup of 2018, the people of Mexico created an earthquake when their national football team scored against Germany, with so many fans jumping up and down at the same time.

The tallest building in the world is called the Burj Khalifa and is a whopping 828 metres high.

As of 2022, the current population of the Earth is estimated to be 7.9 billion people.

Mexico City is sinking at a rate of about 4 inches per year. This is due to the city being constructed on top of a lake.

The first city to reach a population of 1 million was Rome. This happened around the year of 133 B.C.

The surface area of the Earth is around 196,900,000 square miles.

The Earth orbits the sun at an impressive speed of about 70,000 miles per hour.

The Earth completes a full orbit of the sun every 365 days, 5 hours, 48 minutes and 46 seconds. This makes up our calendar year, plus the additional one day that is added every leap year.

The largest island on Earth is Greenland, covering an area of 836,000 square miles.

Many islands grouped together are called an archipelago.

The longest fence ever built can be found in Australia. It measures 5,614 kilometres long and helps to protect farm animals from predators.

The country with the largest population is China. As of 2020, China's population was just over 1.4 billion people.

The busiest beach in the world is in Dalian, China. An average of about 40,000 people visit this beach every day during the summer period.

The full name of Los Angeles is El Pueblo de Nuestra Senora la Reina de Los Angeles de Porcincula.

The most populated country in Africa is Nigeria. Nigeria is home to over 206 million individuals as of 2020.

In 1978, Emilio Palma became the first documented person to have been born in the continent of Antarctica.

The most densely populated nation in the world is Monaco.

Roughly 12% of the world's population live in mountainous areas.

The Chenab Bridge, which is in India, is the highest railway bridge in the world. The bridge passes over the water at a height of nearly 360 metres.

As of 2020, the most popular religion in the world is Christianity, followed by Islam.

The largest port in the world is the port of Shanghai. This is located on the Yangtze River.

The country with the longest railway network is the United States of America. The railway network covers a length of over 250,000 kilometres.

Of all the Caribbean islands, only 1% of them are inhabited.

There are more sheep in the continent of Oceania than there are people.

There are over 300 cities in the world that have a population of over 1 million people.

There are more Italians located in New York City, USA, than there are in Rome, Italy.

As of 2018, the amount of time that it is currently taking the population to double is 46 years.

As of 2019, the current worldwide life expectancy is 72 years. This has steadily been increasing over the past decades.

The country with the highest life expectancy is Hong Kong, with people living there expected to reach over 85 years old.

As of 2019, the country with the lowest life expectancy was the Central African Republic. Average life expectancy there is 53 years.

The largest city in terms of population is Tokyo in Japan. Roughly 37.2 million people currently live in Tokyo.

There is a region in Africa called Bir Tawil that does not belong to any one country. This was due to a dispute over border recognition between the countries of Egypt and Sudan.

The longest direct flight takes just shy of 19 hours, covers 9,537 miles and is from Singapore to New York City.

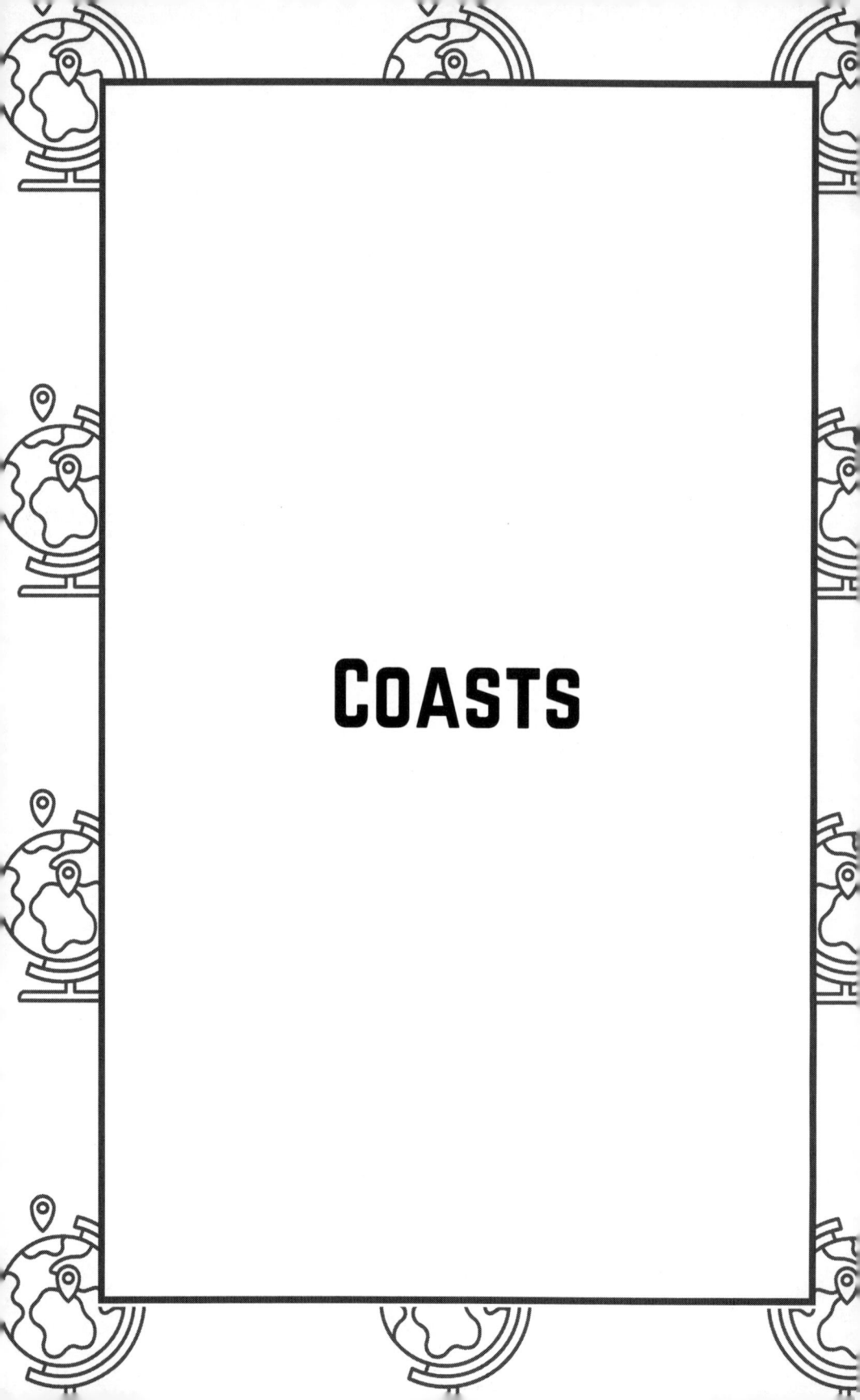

Coasts

COASTS

Precipitation and the Earth's elements can cause erosion to cliff faces. Erosion is where the rock or soil is worn away over time.

Canada has the largest coastline of any country. Canada's coastline is over 150,000 miles long.

If all the coastlines in the world were added together, the length would be 312,000 miles.

Tides are caused by the moon's gravitational force on the Earth.

A big wave can hit cliffs with a pressure of around 500kg per square centimetre. This can be roughly equivalent to a car-sized hammer hitting your finger.

The biggest wave ever documented by humans is said to have reached 524 metres high. This occurred after an earthquake and rockslide in Alaska in 1958.

Storm waves measuring 10 metres high could destroy about 1 metre of cliff face in just one night.

The longest naturally formed beach can be found in Bangladesh. This beach reaches a length of 75 miles.

The longest beach in the world is found in Brazil. Praia do Cassino Beach is around 150 miles long.

Mudflats are often said to smell like rotting eggs. They possess this unfriendly smell due to microbes letting off a gas named hydrogen sulphide.

The largest delta in the world is the Ganges Delta, which covers 41,000 square miles.

Beaches can be very popular places, and at times can be very expensive. Hiring a sun lounger on Waikiki beach in Hawaii can set you back over £40 per day.

Natural Disasters

Natural Disasters

One of the most common ways to measure an earthquake is to use the Richter Scale. This scale measures the magnitude of the earthquake.

The largest earthquake ever recorded was in Chile, in 1960. This earthquake reached 9.5 on the Richter Scale and, unsurprisingly, caused a lot of devastation.

Earthquakes are caused by the movement of tectonic plates that form the Earth's crust.

The study of earthquakes is called "seismology".

As of 2017, about 550 volcanoes had erupted since the beginning of recorded history.

The loudest sound that has ever been recorded was caused by the eruption of a volcano, Krakatoa.

The eruption of Krakatoa, in 1883, was said to have released a similar amount of energy as 15,000 nuclear bombs.

The word "tsunami" is Japanese and translates in English to "great harbour wave".

Tsunamis can travel at very fast speeds. It is possible for them to reach speeds of around 970 kilometres per hour.

The loudest sound that has ever taken place is said have happened when a giant meteor crashed into the ocean 3.5 million years ago. The resulting tsunami went around the Earth several times.

The winds of a tornado can reach speeds of up to 480 kilometres per hour.

Tornadoes are often quite short-lived, with most lasting for less than 10 minutes and travelling 5 to 10 kilometres.

Tornadoes are measured using a scale named the Fujita Scale. This scale ranges from 0 to 5. An F5 is the strongest tornado possible.

The deadliest tornado ever recorded was in Bangladesh in 1989. This tornado killed around 1,300 people and destroyed many villages.

It is possible for tornados to occur over water. When this happens, the phenomenon is called a 'waterspout'.

A category 5 hurricane that hit the United States of America in 2005 caused over $115 billion worth of damage.

Between the years of 2000 and 2012, the many natural disasters that occurred on planet Earth caused damage costing over $1.7 trillion and affected nearly 3 billion people.

The most common type of natural disaster in the USA is flooding. Only around 10% of natural disasters declared by the US president have not been floods.

Around 90% of avalanches are said to have been started by the victim or someone that the victim of the avalanche was with at the time.

Time is crucial when rescuing someone from an avalanche. If you can get them out of the avalanche in less than 15 minutes, then the survival rate is 93%.

For a storm to be upgraded into a hurricane, it needs to have winds that reach speeds of 74 miles per hour or higher for a sustained period.

The largest hailstone ever recorded was nearly 18 centimetres in diameter and weighed just shy of 1 kilogram.

Small earthquakes are happening very frequently. Southern California alone has over 10,000 earthquakes each year. However, most of these are not felt by us humans.

In Cameroon, in 1986, an eruption occurred that released carbon dioxide gas into a nearby village, killing around 1,700 people.

The Chinese famine of 1907 was devastating for many. It is estimated that it caused the deaths of over 24 million people.

Tornadoes have been found in every state in the USA. However, most tornadoes occur in a region called "Tornado Alley" in the central US.

During World War 1 it is estimated that between 40,000 and 80,000 soldiers were killed due to landslides and avalanches that were primarily caused by artillery fire.

Hurricane Audry in 1957 had a storm surge that reached up to 25 miles inland.

Sinkholes can be caused by many factors, such as natural erosion, human mining or excavation under the ground.

Volcanoes are rated on the volcanic explosivity index. The highest rating that a volcano can receive on this index is an 8, which would put the volcano in the category of "supervolcano".

It is estimated that 20 aircraft and 50 boats have been lost to the Bermuda triangle in the last 100 years, with over 1,000 people being killed or remaining unaccounted for.

The Earth

The Earth

There is enough gold within the Earth's inner layers to cover its entire surface.

The Amazon rainforest produces over 20% of the Earth's oxygen. Perhaps we should reconsider cutting so much of it down!

Although home to many dangerous and poisonous animals, the most dangerous animal in Australia is the horse. Roughly 20 people per year die from horse-related injuries.

The tallest waterfall above sea level is Angel Falls in Venezuela. It is 979 metres high.

The tallest waterfall in the world is named the Denmark Strait Cataract. This waterfall is under water and measures 3,505 metres tall.

The word "geography" comes from Greek, and it is broken down to mean "geo" (Earth) and "graphy" (description).

The estimated age of planet Earth is around 4.6 billion years old.

The largest desert in the world (excluding polar deserts) is the Sahara Desert in North Africa. It is over 3 times larger than any other desert and has an area of more than 3.5 million square miles.

The core of the Earth is estimated to be at 6,000 degrees Celsius. This is hotter than the surface of the sun.

The Earth's atmosphere is a gas layer that is around 400 miles in thickness. It is formed primarily of nitrogen and oxygen.

About 6% of the Earth's land surface is covered by rainforests.

Rainforests' canopies can be very thick. It is estimated that it can take some raindrops longer than 10 minutes to hit the rainforest floor after hitting the canopy.

Rainforests receive at least 250 centimetres of rainfall every year, and often much more.

The Amazon rainforest is the largest rainforest on our planet.

If the Amazon rainforest was a country, it would be the 9th largest country on Earth.

One lake, in a rainforest in Dominica, is definitely not suitable for swimming. The temperature of this lake is around 88 degrees Celsius.

About half of all the plants and animals on planet Earth can be found in rainforests.

Rainforests can be found in every continent on the globe apart from the continent of Antarctica, as the weather there is too cold.

There are two types of rainforests: temperate and tropical. Tropical rainforests are the more common of the two.

Around 25% of natural medicines have been discovered within rainforests, which is thanks to their rich biodiversity.

Rainforests are being destroyed at a rapid rate. It is estimated that an area the size of a football pitch is destroyed every six seconds.

In the Arctic regions there is one day a year where it is dark for an entire 24-hour period. Likewise, there is a day every year where it is light for the whole day.

The word for the Arctic comes from the Greek word for bear - "Arktos". This is likely related to the constellations of Ursa Major and Ursa Minor that can be seen in the Arctic skies.

The boiling point of water changes based on your elevation above sea level. The higher you are above sea level, the lower the boiling point.

The only state in the USA that does not possess any documented poisonous snakes is Alaska.

The United States has one tropical rainforest. This is Puerto Rico's El Yunque National Forest.

The country that is said to possess the best quality tap water is Switzerland.

The word "geography" was first used by a scientist named Eratosthenes, who was born in 276 B.C.

Energy cannot be created or destroyed; it can only be transformed from one type of energy to another.

The four seasons that we experience on Earth are caused by the Earth's orbit around the sun and the Earth's tilt on its axis.

The Earth's crust layer varies in thickness from around 10 miles thick to about 125 miles thick in some areas.

Earth is the 3rd closest planet to the sun, with the closest being Mercury.

The Northern Lights, or to give it its scientific name the "aurora borealis", is caused by the Earth's magnetic field and charged particles from the sun.

The lowest recorded point below sea level is the Kola Borehole in Russia. This is how far scientists have managed to go using specialised equipment.

The planet Earth is the fifth largest planet in our solar system. The diameter of the Earth is approximately 12,742 kilometres.

The largest waterfall system in the world is Iguazu Falls. It contains over 275 waterfalls and is shared by Brazil and Argentina.

Over 25% of the world's forests are located in Siberia.

California is the closest US state to Hawaii. However, Hawaii is the furthest US state from California.

Air pollution creates about a third of all toxic contaminants that are found in the ocean.

For a glacier to be called a glacier it needs to be larger than 0.1 square kilometres in size. This may not seem like a large size, however it is the equivalent of around 19 football pitches.

The largest glacier is called the Lambert Glacier. It can be found in Antarctica and is around 270 miles long and 60 miles wide.

If all the glaciers and ice in the world melted, then sea levels would rise by around 80 metres.

The only continent on Earth not to have any glaciers is Oceania.

Some glaciers appear to have a blue colour to them. This is because glacier ice is not able to absorb the colour blue properly.

The Amazon rainforest is very biodiverse. It contains 427 mammal species, 1,300 bird species, over 400 species of amphibians, and 378 species of reptiles. More species are being discovered every year.

Inga Falls, a waterfall in the Democratic Republic of Congo, is the largest waterfall based on the amount of water. It has over 25,000 cubic metres of water travelling down it every second, the same as 10 Olympic size swimming pools.

It is estimated that between 300 and 400 tonnes of pollution enter our rivers and seas every year.

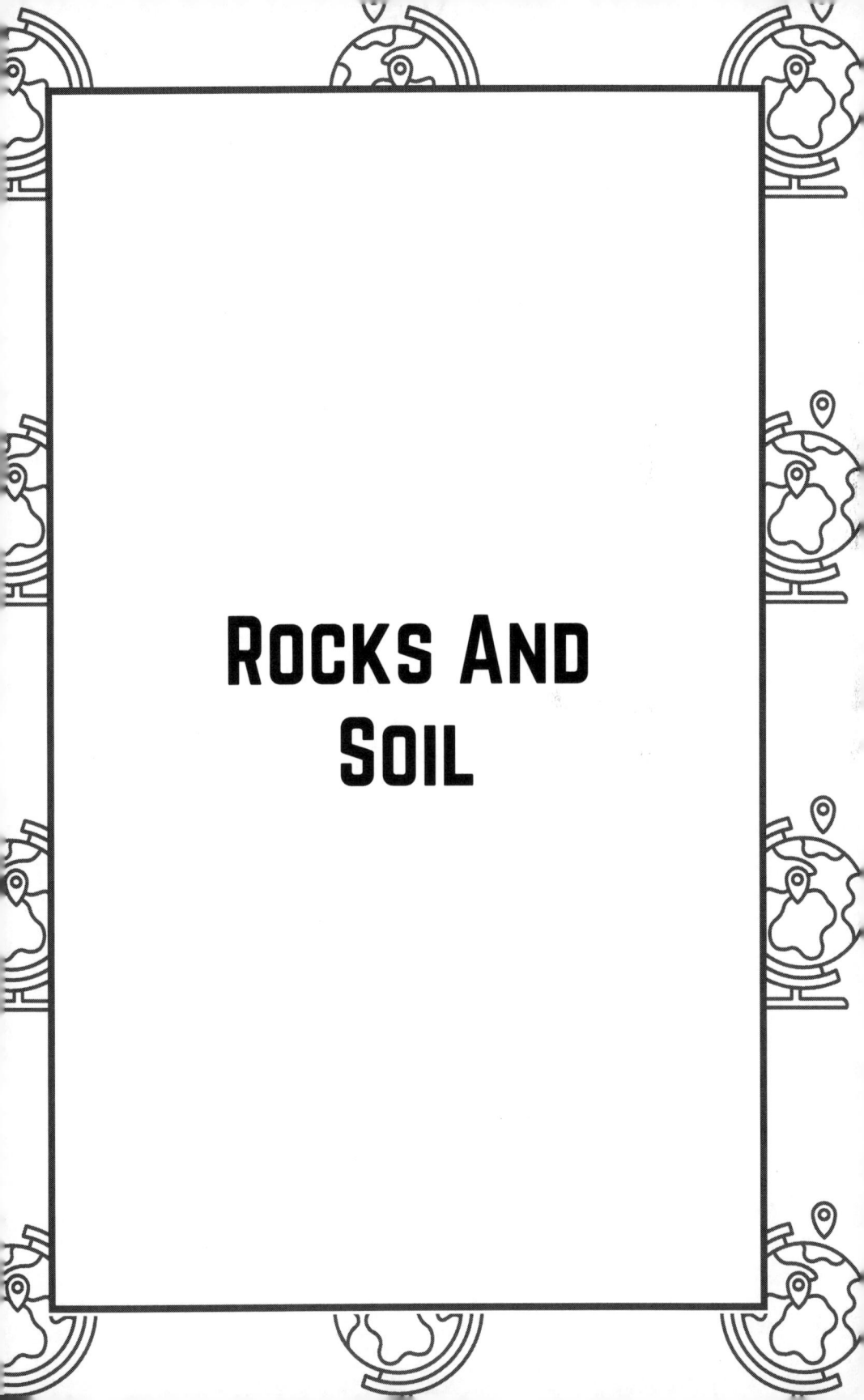

Rocks And Soil

Rocks and Soil

There are over 70,000 different types of soil in the United States of America alone.

There are so many organisms in soil that in just one tablespoon there are more organisms than there are people on the planet.

To form just one inch of topsoil takes a period of over 500 years.

Around 10% of the world's CO2 emissions can be found in soil.

Soils that are healthy have six distinct layers to them.

Although soil may often get overlooked, it is of vital importance to the Earth. 95% of food production relies on soil.

There are three different types of rocks: igneous, metamorphic and sedimentary.

Certain rocks are called ores. This is when the rock contains certain metals, such as gold or silver.

When we think of rocks, we think of strong objects. However, not all rocks are strong. Sand and mud are considered rocks.

The Earth is divided into three main layers. These layers are the core, the mantle and the crust.

Rocks are formed by combinations of different minerals. For example, the minerals that create granite are mica, feldspar and quartz.

The hardest mineral is the diamond.

Fulgurites are created by lightning strikes liquefying silica, sand or rock together.

Rubies and sapphires are composed of the same minerals.

Rubies, sapphires and emeralds are all rarer than diamonds.

Due to the immense air pressure, it is said that the meteor that hit the Earth (that would eventually wipe out the dinosaurs) started making a crater before hitting the Earth's surface.

Printed in Great Britain
by Amazon